# MILLIONS, BILLIONS, & TRILLIONS

## Understanding Big Numbers

by David A. Adler

illustrated by Edward Miller

Holiday House / New York

# One Million is a lot.

It's one thousand thousands. It's written like this: 1,000,000—one followed by six zeroes.

What does one million look like?

Get a bag of granulated sugar, a measuring cup with a ¼ mark on it, and a piece of dark construction paper. Fill the cup with sugar to the ¼ mark. Then carefully spill the sugar from the cup onto the construction paper. You couldn't easily count each granule of sugar on the paper. You are looking at about one million granules of sugar.

How many slices of pizza would one million dollars buy? At two dollars and fifty cents a slice, you could buy two full pies a day for more than sixty-eight years.

Could you count to one million? If you count at a rate of one number a second without stopping, it would take you a little more than eleven and a half days to reach one million.

That's a long time!

One million is a lot.

When people talk about the population of large cities, states, and countries, they often talk in millions. More than eight million people live in New York City.

8,000,000

NEW YORK CITY

More than thirty-seven million people live in California. More than three hundred million people live in the United States.

# One billion is a lot

more than one million. How much is one billion? One billion is one thousand million. It's written like this: 1,000,000,000—one followed by nine zeroes.

1,000,0

Run your fingers through your hair. The average head has one hundred thousand hairs. It would take the heads of ten thousand people together to have about one billion hairs.

0 0,0 0 0

How many ice cream sundaes would one billion dollars buy? At five dollars a sundae, you could buy one thousand sundaes every day for more than five hundred years.

Could you count to one billion? Probably not.

If you count at a rate of one number per second without stopping, it would take you almost thirty-two years to reach one billion.

One billion is a lot.

Many years ago the world's richest people were said to be millionaires. Now they're said to be billionaires.

Someone with one billion dollars could give away ten million dollars every year for one hundred years.

BILLIONAIRE

The world's total population is counted in billions. The world's population is more than seven billion people.

# One trillion is a lot more than one billion. One trillion is one thousand billion. One trillion is one million million. It's written like this:

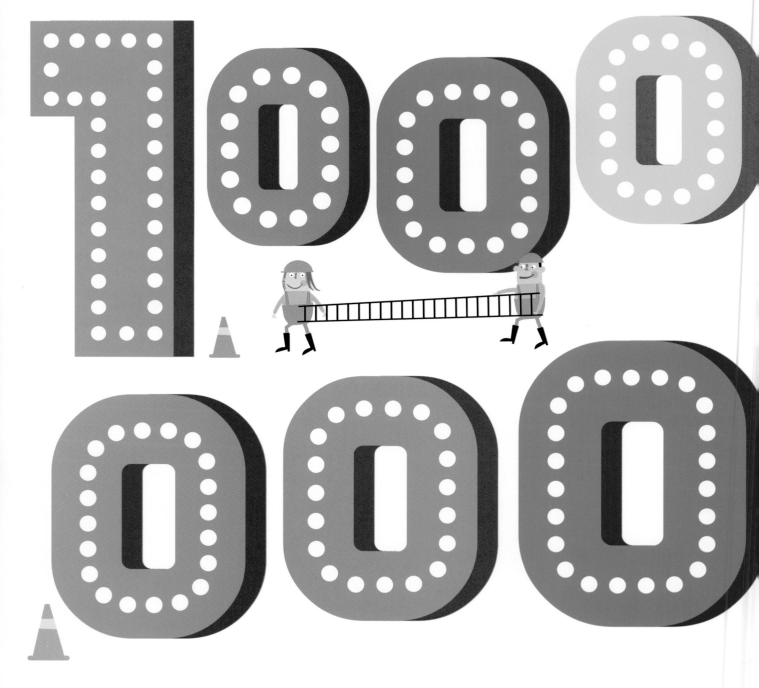

—one followed by twelve zeroes.

It's difficult to imagine a number as large as one trillion.

There are about five hundred popped kernels of popcorn in an average sixteen-ounce bag. One trillion popped kernels would fill two billion bags, enough for about six bags for every person living in the United States.

That's a lot of popcorn!

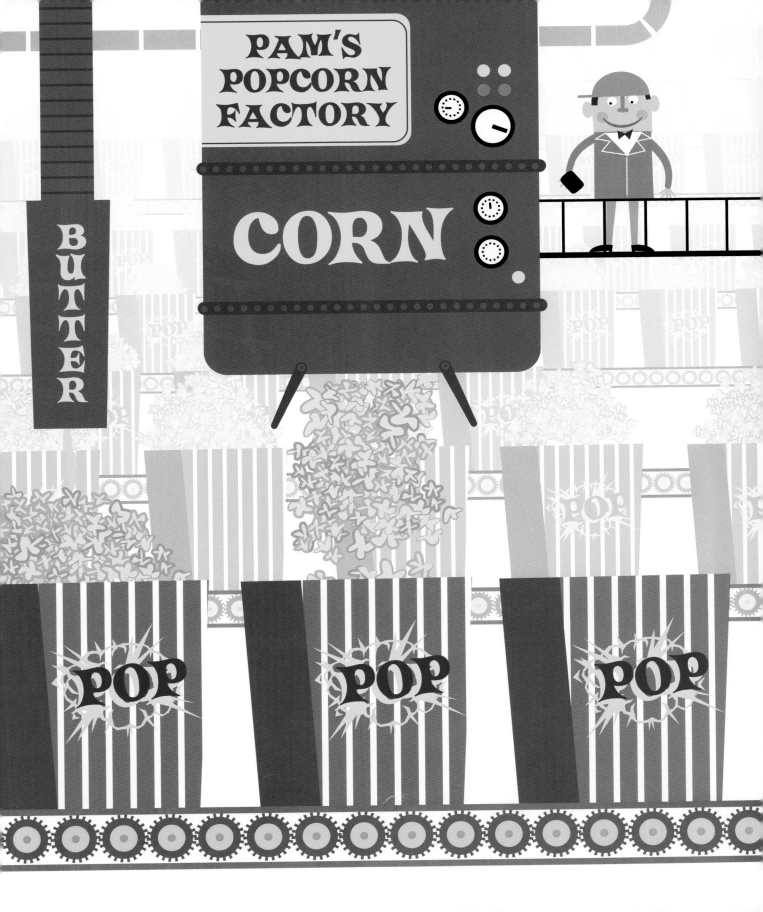

Let's have a birthday party. Let's have lots of birthday parties, one for everyone in the United States under the age of fifteen. Let's have pizza, cake, ice cream, and a magician at each party.

At two hundred and fifty dollars a party, with one trillion dollars, we could do that every year for about sixty years.

Hocus-
pocus!

Try to imagine a stack of one-hundred-dollar bills. One trillion dollars would make a stack about seven hundred miles high.

You couldn't count to a trillion.

The amount of money the United States government spends each year and the amount it owes are measured in trillions.

The total of all the coins and paper currency in the world is about five trillion dollars: $5,000,000,000,000.

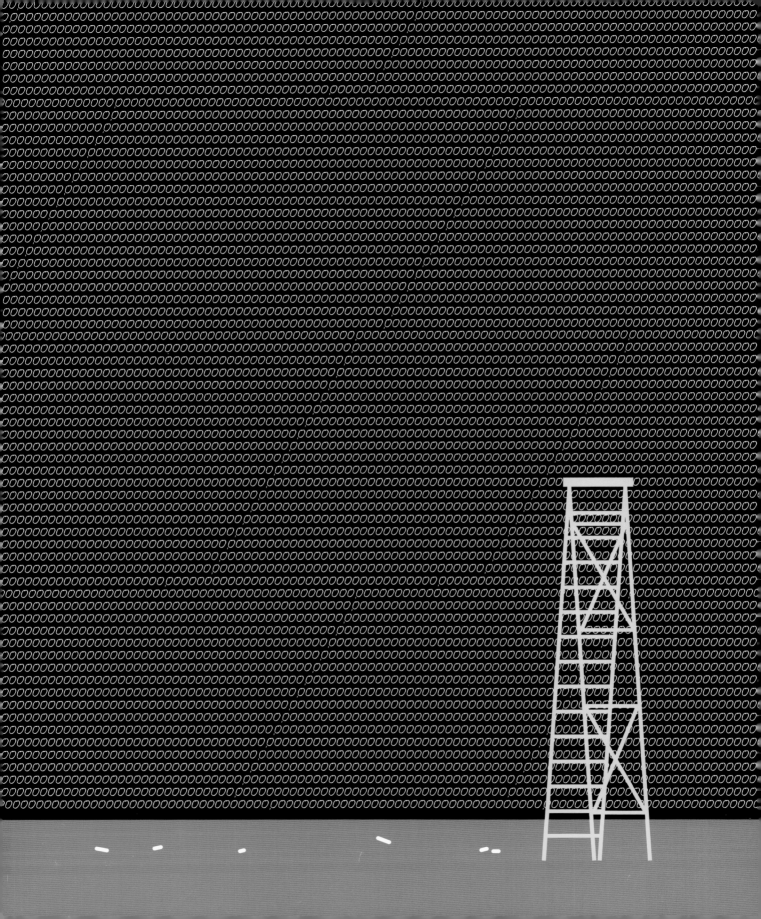

Counting to a million would take days.
Counting to a billion would take years. And
counting to a trillion would be impossible.
But when people talk about the population of
large countries, it's good to know how much
a million and a billion are. When politicians
talk about how much our government spends
and how much money it owes, it's good to
know how much a trillion is.

It's important to know about large numbers
such as millions, billions, and trillions.

## Author's Note

A million is a lot. A billion is more than a million. A trillion is even more than that. And there are numbers even greater than a trillion.

One thousand trillion is a **quadrillion**. It's written like this:

# 1,000,000,000

—one followed by fifteen zeroes.

One million trillion is a **quintillion**. It's written like this:

# 1,000,000,000

—one followed by eighteen zeroes.

One billion trillion is a **sextillion**. It's written like this:

# 1,000,000,000

—one followed by twenty-one zeroes.

If you counted by millions—one million, two million, three million—and added one million each second, it would take more than thirty million years to reach a sextillion.

00,000

00,000,000

00,000,000,000

What if something is beyond being counted? What if it would be impossible to even guess its number? Anything that numerous is said to be **infinite**.

The names for large numbers are not the same everywhere. In some parts of the world, what we call a billion is called a milliard. What we call a trillion is called a billion. What we call a quadrillion is called a billiard. What we call a quintillion is called a trillion. What we call a sextillion is called a quadrillion.

For my brother Nathan,
who works daily with large numbers

This book meets the Common Core State Standards
for fourth-grade mathematics in Number and Operations
in Base Ten (4.NBT.1)

Text copyright © 2013 by David A. Adler
Illustrations copyright © 2013 by Edward Miller III
All Rights Reserved
HOLIDAY HOUSE is registered in the U.S. Patent and Trademark Office.
Printed and Bound in July 2013 at Toppan Leefung, DongGuan City, China.
www.holidayhouse.com
3 5 7 9 10 8 6 4 2
Library of Congress Cataloging-in-Publication Data
Adler, David A.
Millions, billions, & trillions: understanding big numbers / by David A. Adler ; illustrated by Edward Miller. — 1st ed.
p. cm.
ISBN 978-0-8234-2403-0 (hardcover)
1. Number concept—Juvenile literature. 2. Million (The number)—Juvenile literature.
3. Billion (The number)—Juvenile literature. 4. Trillion (The number)—Juvenile literature.
I. Miller, Edward, 1964- ill. II. Title.
QA141.15.A35 2012
513—dc23
2011044752

ISBN 978-0-8234-3049-9 (paperback)

Visit www.davidaadler.com for more information on the author, for a list of his books, and to download teacher's guides and educational materials. You can also learn more about the writing process, take fun quizzes, and read select pages from David A. Adler's books.

Visit www.edmiller.com for more information on the illustrator and a list of his books.